YOUR MAGICAL BRAIN
How It Learns Best

Teaching with Brain-based Learning principles
in the classroom and at home.

Gary Anaka
Brain-based Learning Facilitator

Portal Press

Portal Press
Vancouver BC
hgreavesster@gmail.com

Copyright © 2005 Gary Anaka
Revised edition 2011
Reprinted 2014
Reprinted 2015

Anaka, Gary 1948
Your Magical Brain: How It Learns Best

Every effort has been made to trace the critical source of text
and other material. Where the attempt has been unsuccessful,
the publisher would be pleased to hear from copyright holders
to rectify any errors or omissions.

Portal Press books are available at special discounts for bulk
purchases by corporations, institutions and other organizations.
For more information, please contact the Special Markets
Department at Portal Press hgreavesster@gmail.com

ISBN 978-0-921138-03-7

Editorial Coordination: Howard Greaves
Page Layout: Intelliga Designs
Artist: Barb Murphy
Printed in Canada

Contents

CHAPTER 7: The Teenage Brain

Acknowledgements

I am very grateful for the Brain-based Learning Facilitator's training that I have received for the last 15 years. I would especially like to thank Eric Jensen for all the levels of training he provides from the Jensen Learning Corporation. I would like to acknowledge the ongoing support of my publisher, Howard Greaves. I would also like to thank the students, parents and my fellow colleagues for consistent positive feedback over the years. Most of all, I would like to thank my loving wife, Maureen Anaka, for her expertise and endless loving support.

**The Only Space We Have To Conquer
Is That Between Our Own Ears!**

Foreward

Today's schools are full of students struggling with learning difficulties, boredom or stress. It is getting harder to reach and engage students. Improvement and renewal are certainly needed. Progressive teachers and leading-edge schools are reassessing their thinking about how we learn. Teachers can no longer just teach, test and hope for the best. New ideas are continually coming from Applied Educational Neuroscience. For the first time in history, the brain's activity can be measured and studied while we are still alive.

Brain-based learning does not come from a single discipline. It draws from a host of sciences such as nutrition, chemistry, biology, cognitive science, social neuroscience and others to form an interdisciplinary approach to learning. Opportunities for teachers and parents to discover and implement new, simple and successful teaching strategies are available.

I was a Learning Assistance specialist with over 32 years of classroom experience. In 1997, I completely retrained in the new field of brain-based learning. Success! Brain-based learning offered tremendous hope and optimism for the future. Teachers, early childhood educators, students, parents, adults and seniors can also benefit from this new way of understanding about how the brain learns best naturally.

When I discovered brain-based learning my life changed completely as a professional educator and human being. In the classroom my students loved the brain-based learning approach. Discipline problems decreased considerably. My students became more engaged and motivated. Brain-based learning offered me endless opportunities to become a more highly effective teacher and parent.

What can brain-based learning strategies offer you? When applied, they make learning easier for your students, keep them engaged with school, boost achievement and cut down on motivational problems and behaviour issues. Teaching smarter will ignite or re-ignite a natural love of learning. What teachers have always known intuitively has been validated and the rewards are great. Enjoy a renewed interest in your job.

This resource book provides 100% practical, non-technical, classroom proven brain-based learning strategies. Easy, ready-to-use, teacher-friendly formats are described. Your Magical Brain: How It Learns Best is all about maximizing teaching and learning in the classroom, making it easier for the teacher to teach and making it easier for the student to learn. What could be more hopeful!

Some Guiding Principles of Brain-based Learning
(random order)

☑ No two brains are alike.

☑ The brain is built for survival.

☑ The brain is constantly trying to make meaning.

☑ The brain is a powerful information processor.

☑ Good brain health requires proper nutrition, exercise, adequate amounts of sleep and sufficient intake of water. These put the brain in an optimal condition for learning.

☑ Stress and threats reduce the potential for learning. The brain moves into survival mode at the expense of higher-order thinking.

☑ The human brain is a social brain. A sense of community is fundamentally important. Learning occurs through communication and cooperation with others.

☑ Movement and physical activity grow a better brain. The amount of exercise we get has a huge effect upon our ability to think, learn and remember.

☑ An enriched environment creates an enriched brain. Enrichment is a critical requirement for wiring the brain at any age.

☑ The brain learns in many ways (learning styles). Students need to know what their individual style is and how to develop it.

☑ The brain is not designed for constant attention.

☑ The brain thrives on novelty. Novelty is a big attention-grabber.

☑ Repetition strengthens the brain (unless it is boring).

☑ New concepts are best learned by connecting them to prior knowledge.

☑ The brain excels when solving real life problems.

☑ Emotions strongly influence attention, learning and memory. Emotions cannot be ignored. Positive emotional states are essential.

☑ The best memories are formed when the brain is involved in doing something.

☑ The brain learns best with personal experiences, patterns and general themes.

☑ Feedback is essential for survival.

☑ Relaxed alertness is a top-notch state for learning. Fear needs to be eliminated.

☑ Learning is mind and body together, our whole self.

Chapter 1

Nourishing the Brain

In terms of biological needs, your brain requires essential elements to operate every single moment of your life. Living in our increasingly complex, technical world requires a lot of brain power. Without it, we cannot learn or reach our potentials. The first step on the path of learning is to nourish the brain.

1.1 Movement is KING

It is an anatomical and physiological fact that our bodies are not meant to be stationary. Throughout thousands of years of evolution, humans have been engineered for movement. We are not designed to sit for long periods of time, at any age.

Did you know that your brain does not store energy? It constantly runs on empty. A fresh supply of blood brings in oxygen and glucose that the brain needs to operate. If the brain does not have enough energy, students become restless, listless or bored. Therefore teachers need to incorporate active exercise into their daily routines. Learning requires energy.

Movement opens up endless possibilities for influencing learners. Movement facilitates cognition. Here are some of the wonderful things that can happen when a body is in motion: heart-rate increases, circulation improves, stress is relieved, feeling good endorphins are released and memory is enhanced. Plus, endless irrelevant information is blocked out more effectively making it easier to pay attention and focus. Exercise and moving literally build up brain circuits. More brain circuits means more brainpower.

If movement facilitates cognition, then why not do math, grammar or spelling while on the move? Why not learn using your body? It's way more interesting and engaging than just sitting and listening, or doing board work. Your body is full of millions and millions of cells. Engage those cells because they have a memory of their own. When you learn something with your body you remember it with less effort. Studies show that students who exercise outperform those who don't.

You'll find that when you get your students to move, magic occurs. Their whole mind, body and spirit will be engaged in the academic learning process. Students will be ready and more willing to tackle new information and new challenges. Moving fires up learning, overcomes fatigue, drowsiness, and deadly routines.

Eliminate those blank stares. Research clearly states that people cannot pay attention for long periods of time. If something does not occur that is different, the mind begins to wander. Prolonged periods of direct attention lead to longer periods of inattention.

Also, when the brain gets too many stimuli, it gets fatigued and fails to focus. Therefore, students need to be taught with instructional methods that alternate between active learning activities and sedentary learning activities.

There is nothing wrong with classrooms full of students in motion. That's the way the brain learns best naturally. Classrooms, equipped with balance balls to sit on instead of chairs, exercise bikes, mini trampolines or simple gym equipment for students to use, are brain compatible. Give your students a physical and mental workout. The bottom line is: movement engages learners.

> # What makes us move is what makes us think!

1.2 Oxygen

Oxygen is vital to the brain's survival. It cannot learn without oxygen. The brain is only a small part of the body's weight but it can use up to 20% of the body's oxygen.

Clean fresh air is essential for young people and you. That's why a regular exercise program is crucial to get oxygen into our bodies and brains. Exercise increases the blood flow, heart rate and breathing rate supplying oxygen to the brain. Are you meeting the most basic of all human needs for your students? Think of your own classroom, your own workplace. What is the air quality like? Ever taught in an old portable? Open the windows whenever possible.

1.3 Water

Hydration issues are huge. Did you know that your brain is mostly water: 75 to 80%? Water is vital to life and to your brain. It is the secret player in the great mystery of learning. Learning and thinking are hard to do if the brain is dehydrated. Students who have dehydrated or partially hydrated brains may well have learning difficulties. Brain cells talk to each other with electrical transmissions within the nervous system. Water is vital for this chemical process.

Water delivers oxygen to the brain cells. It aids in digesting foods. It is essential for the development of nerves and critical to mental and physical performance. Unlike other beverages, no digestion is needed. Brains that are well hydrated create excellent neurotransmissions. Brains that are well hydrated reduce stress.

Nourishing the brain requires everyone to drink clear water all day long. Pop, power drinks, coffee and juices are not clear water.

It's best to drink room temperature water instead of cold water so that extra washroom visits can be eliminated. A top strategy is to sip water all day long. The significance of water cannot be underestimated. Water is food!

1.4 Diet

Glucose fuels the brain. Being smart means being smart about what you eat. Right across the social economic spectrum, experience tells us that good diet choices are not always the case! There is an enormous ongoing need to give students and parents information about nutrition – especially about how to feed a brain. Healthy food will boost performance, supply energy and allow students to concentrate.

Kids need to be coached at an early age about life supporting nutritional habits. They need to know the brain will not function well on a diet of junk food, food additives, sugar or chemicals. Avoid eating anything that has a long list of incomprehensible ingredients. Avoid eating packaged foods. Our bodies and brains do not run well on inadequate or poor nutrition.

Breakfast is the most important meal of the day. After a night's sleep, your brain needs fuel if it wants to have power for the day. An ideal breakfast is a combination of foods that give a sustained energy source. A superior breakfast would be: fresh fruit or fruit juice, protein and whole grains. Brainpower requires protein for breakfast. Eat carbohydrates after school because they can create drowsiness.

What is the number one brain food? Fish! Fish contains a special fat called Omega-3. There is a need to get Omega-3 from our diet as the body does not produce it naturally. Omega-3 can also be obtained from flax seeds, hemp seeds, avocados, olive oil and walnuts.

Next, eat antioxidants. Blueberries are highly recommended for their antioxidant effect protecting the brain from stress damage. Blueberries are in a new family of foods that nutritionists call brain berries. Raspberries, strawberries, huckleberries, blackberries and currants are all part of this family.

Enjoy wholesome foods. Everyday go for a variety of vegetables, fruits, nuts and whole grains. Be sure to have a least five servings of fruits and vegetables daily to supply vitamins and minerals essential for learning, memory and intelligence. Eat eggs because eggs are good for supporting your memory. Eat lean proteins to think better and boost your mental performance.

It makes a lot of sense to get kids involved in growing and preparing food. They are more likely to eat what they produce and create.

Eat from the rainbow

Serious consideration should be given to protect young and growing brains by supplementing with vitamins. The B vitamins are essential for the growth of neurons and for protecting the brain from stress. B vitamins synthesize neurotransmitters supporting thinking and memory. Vitamin C is absolutely essential for the brain. Vitamin C plays a major role in brain biochemistry and is a superstar brain booster and preserver. Vitamin D also protects and preserves brain cells. Young children and adolescent brains are always hungry. To support the growing brain give it what it needs to function at peak levels. Small investments can mean lifelong returns. Vitamins are life insurance.

Everyone can benefit from becoming more nutritionally wise. Do some research and get more informed. It's obvious that a well nourished brain can learn easier and more efficiently. Brain nourishment is vital. One of the primary principles of brain-based learning is to nourish the brain with copious amounts of oxygen, water and nutritious food for proper brain functioning. Feed that brain!

2

CHAPTER

How the Brain Works Best

Making learning a fun and unforgettable experience requires a firm grounding in how the brain operates. If you want to increase student motivation and raise academic success, then there is a need to know what goes on in the brain. Here is a brief and relevant overview of how we can make learning occur easier and more often.

2.1 Safety

The basic instinct of the human brain is to survive. Survival issues always come first. The brain needs safety to function. Stress and threats disrupt learning. Classrooms, workplaces and home environments, for that matter, must be free of any kind of threat. When the brain perceives danger, it is less capable of making judgments, recording information, solving problems, creating, paying attention or performing higher-order skills. When a student does not feel safe, there is no interest in paying attention to the teacher or the material being presented because the brain is on high alert, ready to run. That's survival mode. Learning cannot occur unless you feel safe.

This is what happens to all of us each moment of the day. Whenever you enter a new situation or meet a new person, the brain makes an immediate microsecond analysis. Is this person a threat? Or is this person a reward? How do you present yourself to your students?

2.2 Upshift vs Downshift

Information from our senses is constantly coming into our brain. If this information is non-threatening, upshifting will occur.

Upshifting happens like this. Sensory information travels to the center of the brain to the **thalamus**. The thalamus acts like a relay switch sorting out thousands of impressions per hour. If the information is non-threatening, the thalamus then relays the information to the **hippocampus**. The hippocampus is a tiny organ in the brain responsible for making memory. The messages are then sent to the neocortex at the top of the brain where evaluation and interpretation occur. The process is slow. Analysis and decisions are made when the brain is engaged in an upshift position. That's where all learners need to be.

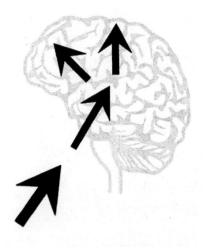

upshifting

On the other hand, threats or stress downshift the brain. A little bit of stress is good for learning. Too much stress becomes distress and therefore a threat. Since the brain's number one job is to survive, it immediately shifts into survival mode when it is threatened. The body is ready for fight or flight. This effect is called downshifting and the response is automatic and fast. Downshifting is a biological response of the brain to a fear, real or perceived.

Downshifting happens like this. Information comes into the brain and enters the thalamus. A threat is perceived. The threat is immediately transferred to the **amygdala**. The amygdala is an organ in the brain that is the seat of our emotions. It is also our fear center. The brain registers DANGER. Responses are then transferred down to the back of the brain. The survival system has taken over. Logic, reasoning and thinking have stopped. The brain is now downshifted. Amygdala attacks cause trouble with focusing on anything not directly related to survival. When you are afraid you cannot think straight. You just want to run. This is not where you want your learners to be.

I call this brain hijacking. It occurs in classrooms in schools everyday. Teachers must make efforts to identify any sources of threats and help prevent them. As well, teachers must be careful not to downshift their students. A safe, non-threatening environment is critical. This is a key principle for brain compatible teaching and learning. Brains must be safe. That means no bullying, no putdowns, and no threats in classrooms, hallways and schoolyards. Brain compatible schools are a safe community, a large extended family that does more than deliver content and provide certification.

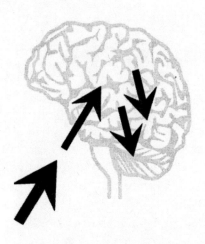

downshifting

2.3 Information Processor

What do you think your brain is constantly doing? It is trying to make meaning. Meaning-making is far more essential to the brain than learning facts, statistics, theories or random data. The search to make meaning of life's experiences is paramount. The brain wants to understand what is going on. It seeks to know. It seeks to understand. It's trying to predict what's going to happen next.

2.4 The Reticular Activating System (RAS)

There is a system in your brain that pays attention. It is a sorting arrangement. It decides which stimulus to focus on. It's like radar antenna, signaling a wake-up call that is getting us ready to respond to our environment. The RAS is the "HOOK".

A few years ago I was doing many workshops out of town and I needed a new truck. My son and I decided that a big, white pickup truck would be perfect. That morning as we were driving to school, what did we notice? The exact size and color of truck that we had agreed upon was all around us. What happened? We had programmed our reticular activating system to be on the lookout for that particular truck. So it didn't take long to find the one we were interested in. It was on our radar screen.

If something is **relevant** to you, your brain will focus and pay attention because it's important. Learning occurs when the RAS is engaged. Learning is about turning this system on and keeping it on.

2.5 Brain States

Learning starts here! **Managing states is the biggest daily job a teacher has to do.** It's a critical job, individually, collectively and personally. Unfortunately, not much is known about brain states and how significant they are.

Teaching and learning are more than just delivering content with time honoured strategies. To increase attention and retention, to advance knowledge, to support students to learn, you have to understand that learning is **state dependent**.

What are brain states? Brain states are a combination of your health, your moods, your chemistry and your thoughts representing how you feel at any given moment. There are learning states and non-learning states. Non-learning states are endless in number. Boredom, apathy, frustration, distress, tiredness, apprehension, listlessness, indifference, lethargy, sluggishness, disinterest, discontent and inertia are just a few examples. These are not receptive states for learning and the chances are very good that learning will not occur when someone is feeling like that.

How do you know what kind of state someone is in? Your clues are modeled in the outer world by behaviours. If you see a student who is completely bored and disengaged from learning, then your opportunity to change the brain state to support them is at hand. Go to work. Time for a state changer.

Paying attention and motivation are really the same thing. They activate brain processes allowing for the selection of new information. High contrast, originality and exciting events create excellent brain states. Endless worksheets, notes off the board, lectures and grinding through huge textbooks page after page, do not.

Our attention system can be restarted by managing states. State changers are ideal to maintain the learner's attention. The good news is that state changers are free, easy to do and take little time to prepare. They don't have to be complex or lengthy to be effective.

Learning to manage brain states is a key to effective teaching in today's world. If students are not in a learning state, then why continue to teach or ask them to do things they don't respond to. For years and years, my training evolved around a simple principle. If student behaviour is not appropriate and if students are not paying attention then **change their state**. You can make a huge difference in the classroom and at home by being aware of the top brain states.

2.6 Top Brain States

Paying attention, of course, is a big deal. Studies have shown that a lot of the teacher's time in classrooms on a daily basis is just spent getting students to pay attention.

A highly effective way to put students in a learning state is to ask questions. Questioning is in line with how the brain learns best. Asking questions turns on the RAS and wakes up the brain. Since the brain is always trying to make meaning, it naturally responds to questions. How many times a day do you challenge your students with questions?

Who, what, where, when, and how questions launch the brain into a mode of creating new ideas and predicting the future. The superstar question to ask is **"What if?"**. What if summer never ended? What if frogs could fly? What if you woke up tomorrow and you were a genius? The brain is especially engaged when it is guessing. Student generated questions are the best of all.

Top brain states are created through:

- ✓ movement and exercise
- ✓ questions
- ✓ curiosity
- ✓ anticipation
- ✓ challenge
- ✓ relaxed alertness

2.7 Learning Styles

Ways of receiving information are called learning styles. There are three major modes of learning:

a) **Visual** (learning by seeing). Good visual learners tend to learn best by seeing pictures, movies, maps, charts, diagrams, etc.

b) **Auditory** (learning by hearing). Auditory learners like to listen to music, talk on the telephone, discuss things and describe things verbally.

c) **Kinesthetic** (learning by doing, moving or touching). Kinesthetic learners love to learn with first-hand experience. They learn best by actually doing. Hands-on learning is what Mother Nature designed for them. Sitting still for long extended periods of time is difficult for them because they want action.

Think about school for a moment. Even from the first grades there are kids who sit quietly writing, reading and learning their lessons. They get the rewards. Then, there are kids who talk a lot and tend to be noisier. They are the ones who are asked to keep quiet. And finally, there are the kids who fidget, squirm, twitch, wiggle and just have trouble sitting still. These students are often considered problem children.

It would be very unusual to find someone that only uses one learning style. For example, I am a visual-kinesthetic learner. If I want to remember something, then I need to write it down or make a sketch. I also love to do things with my hands.

Since students receive information in different ways, this can lead to serious problems in the classroom and at home. If a student receives information best visually and the teacher gives information orally, then the student is at a disadvantage.

Learner problems can be teacher generated. A teacher, who repeatedly delivers the same type of lesson, day in and day out, is not supporting the learning situation. The solution is to honour diversity in the classroom.

Student complaints, that some teachers do the same old thing lesson after lesson, are often justified. Teachers can be the generators of apathy, boredom or discontent. How we teach makes a big difference as to whether students are eager to learn in our class or just tune out. If students learn in different ways, teachers need to teach in different ways.

Finally, make sure students know their own personal learning style. If students want to learn some material easily, quickly and efficiently, then they need to hear it, see it and feel it every time. Learning occurs best by studying in multiple ways not just in one preferred style. Use all three learning styles in the classroom and encourage parents to do the same at home.

2.8 Plasticity

Only a few years ago it was believed that the brain could not change. Today, what we know about brain plasticity is the new hope for the future. How does the brain learn? It learns by physically changing itself.

The brain is plastic and malleable. Every time you learn something new a change has occurred in the brain circuits. This change is called plasticity. We have all learned to do thousands and thousands of things over a lifetime. The brain changes every single time we learn a new skill, a new ability or gain a new idea. Getting smarter means the brain is making new connections.

Changes that the brain has made since birth are massive. At a very early age, children learn to master many, many different skills. As they learn these new skills, the connections between brain cells grow, expand, remodel and reshape. The brain is customizing those new skills to fit in with its already existing neural pathways. Experiences build a totally unique brain.

Your brain changes absolutely every single day regardless of your age. The connections and the patterns between neurons alter on a daily basis. That means learning difficulties can be overcome, injuries can be overcome and the brain can heal itself. Teachers need to believe in plasticity.

2.9 Brain Chemistry

Switches that control brain plasticity are chemicals called **neurotransmitters**. Neurotransmitters are how brain cells talk to each other. They are the biochemical messengers that start activity or stop activity in the brain. Brain chemicals are the highways that carry your thoughts and feelings.

Neurotransmitters enable learning and memory to occur. They contribute to the learning process in many different ways. Here are two of the key brain chemicals required for learning.

Serotonin: Serotonin is your brain's mood regulator, the soothing chemical. When you are feeling good and happy, levels of serotonin are up. Serotonin promotes optimism, keeps us calm and relaxed, cuts stress and regulates sleep. It is critical for memory formation and is necessary for learning.

Dopamine: This neurochemical controls energy levels – the release of energy, consumption of energy and the production of energy. Dopamine plays a huge role in focusing attention. It is our all time, feeling good brain chemical that provides us with rewards. We all love dopamine because it feels good.

When a student is greeted by a teacher wearing a smile, the student can experience:

- a reward
- a safe feeling
- the release of serotonin and dopamine
- a potential for engagement
- an upshifted brain

Turn the book upside down and observe the teacher. When a student is greeted by a scowl or a frown, the student can experience:

- a threat
- a fight or flight response
- a loss of executive functions
- a flood of stress chemicals
- a downshifted brain

Teachers have a huge impact on the learning process

2.10 Brain Gym ®

One of the most effective teaching strategies available to anyone is Brain Gym. Brain Gym is being practised in the most forward moving classrooms and schools around the world. It can be done anywhere, at anytime with any age group of any ability level. No equipment is required.

Brain Gym is awesome! In every single lesson, workshop, training or keynote presentation that I do for teachers and the general public, I start with Brain Gym. I want my audiences to be upshifted, alert and ready to listen and learn.

Brain friendly instruction requires brain friendly teaching strategies. Brain Gym delivers it. It's very simple. The movements are effective for any student getting them ready to learn. Over the years the vast majority of my students have told me, over and over again, how much they enjoy doing Brain Gym exercises. Brain Gym supports and helps students to succeed.

Brain Gym has only a few dozen movements. The best and easiest are called cross-laterals or crossovers. They wake up the brain. Crossovers balance the right and left hemispheres of the brain so that both sides can communicate or cross talk with each other.

Cross-laterals are best done standing but can also be done sitting if there is a physical challenge. Here is how to do them. Reach across and touch your right elbow with your left hand. Alternatively, touch your left elbow with your right hand. Do this slowly and rhythmically 20 times or more. Crossovers involve touching ankles, shoulders or knees. Crossovers improve mental performance getting brains engaged and energized. What could be easier?

These simple, learning readiness sequences done at the start of the school day or during class help manage student states. If students are not alert, then a state change is needed. It's up to the teacher to manage the situation and get kids moving. State management, through orchestrated movements like Brain Gym, is a great way to boost student achievement. Want to help overcome the burgeoning problem of passivity? Want to change your student's brain states on the spot? Get them moving with Brain Gym. It's fun and it's free.

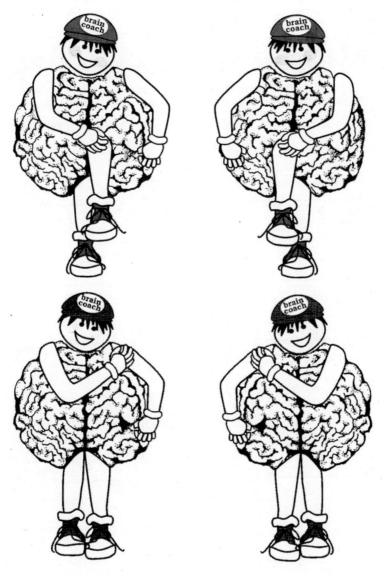

2.11 The 'Captain' of the Ship

Place your fingers on your forehead. You have just made contact with the prefrontal cortex, the 'Captain' of your ship. Your 'Captain' is your thinker, organizer, planner, the executive center of your brain. Why do we go to school? Why do we have to study all kinds of subjects year after year? The ultimate reason is to grow your prefrontal cortex so that you can function successfully in life. Going to school is all about growing the 'Captain'.

How do you hook in students of all ages regardless of subject material? In all my years of teaching, the brain was the hottest topic I ever taught. That's because everybody was on the same page. Everyone owns a brain and brain research is opening up awesome fantastic realities that we never dreamed about. A new renaissance in learning is sweeping the world and the old paradigms are dying. At the core of this is the reality that your little 3 pound wonder is the most valuable thing you own. That makes brain research totally relevant and real.

So, for the students, the purpose for the worksheet, the paragraph, the P.E. class, the test, the unit, the curriculum is to support the growth of their 'Captain'. How can anyone argue with that?

BRAIN STARTERS

Maintain good connections between brain neurons and...

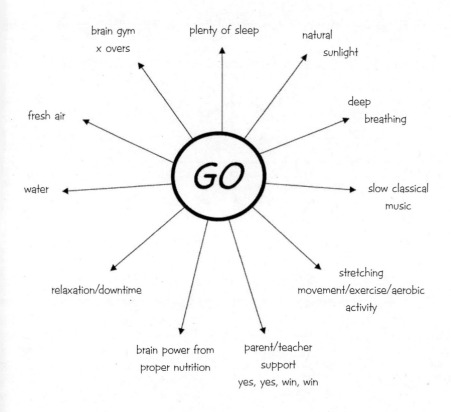

support learning

BRAIN BLOCKERS

Hinder the neurons from working and...

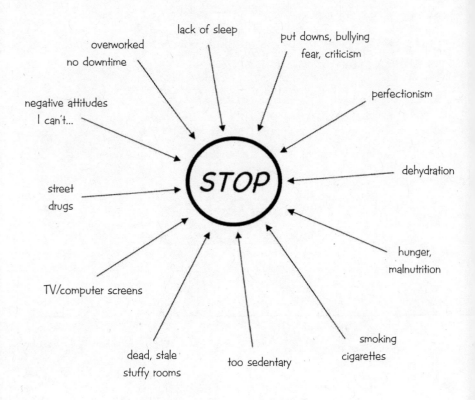

prevent learning

Brain Compatible Instruction Strategies

Great effective teachers do more than just show and tell or give lectures. They engage, involve and constantly shift their instructional strategies. Here are 15 highly practical strategies that can make your classrooms come alive. These strategies are applicable to any activity and can easily be adapted to any age level. They are active, top-notch teaching tools that can help you succeed with every learner.

.

3.1 Unique brains

No two brains are alike. Your brain has been customizing itself ever since the day you were born. It works well for you because you have encouraged it to develop to meet your precise needs. Your brain is just right for you.

Students have different learning styles, different strengths and weaknesses, different developmental stages and a wide range of abilities and experiences. Thirty plus individual brains are hard to deal with all at the same time. Classrooms around the world are full of these challenges. It's not possible to prepare a lesson that suits every single member of your class. But, everyone in your class owns a brain. Embracing brain-based learning principles is a great leap forward supporting educators to reach all students in the class, including the hard to reach. Honour the reality that everyone is different. No two brains are alike.

3.2 Rituals

How do you start your lessons? Are you able to start on time? Do you spend a lot of effort getting your students to settle down? Do you find yourself saying things like "sit down", "turn around", "take out your books" or "let's get ready to go". That old approach wastes a lot of time and energy.

Why not get your class focused and on track instantly? Opening rituals are the answer. Rituals can involve movement, a greeting or an acknowledgement. The following strategy worked and I did it for years. When the bell rang to start the class, I got my students to raise their hands, stand up and exchange high fives with their classmates. Then, while standing we all did Brain Gym for a few minutes. Why?

The brain loves rituals. Rituals provide a feeling of safety and they are welcoming. There is no competition. Everyone is equal. Every student in the class, including me, moved together to begin the lesson. This was a significant part of my daily classroom procedure. Students were put in a positive learning state instantly. Opening rituals are an enormously effective strategy to begin every lesson.

Better yet, get the students to do the opening ritual. Let them evolve their own such as a song, a cheer or a rhyme. The goal is to have the students feeling good and feeling safe, ready to learn.

Use closing rituals instead of letting the class just die out, waiting for the bell. Rituals build a positive community in your classroom taking only a few, cost free seconds. Rituals are awesome state changers.

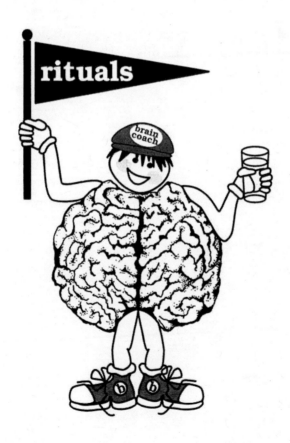

3.3 Downtime

The human brain is not designed for constant input. When we learn something new, we cannot consciously process it fast enough to remember it right away. Meaning comes from internal processing. A constant flow of new information needs to stop coming in so that the new material can be sorted, filed and imprinted in the memory banks. Input, input, input simply overloads the brain.

Learning is a complicated process and takes up a lot of brain resources. There are limitations on how many resources that can be used at one time. The brain needs to break and pause when learning new material. Therefore, downtime is needed for permanent installation in the memory bank.

What does this mean for teachers? Purposeful downtime needs to be given throughout the day. It's crucial for long-term memory formation, reducing fatigue and boosting cognition. This reflects our natural learning cycles of tension and then relaxation. How do you schedule downtime in your classroom, on the job or at home?

Tips: Downtime can involve state changers, energizers, movement, group discussions, reflection, drawing, sketching, humour, music, deep breathing, quiet time, etc.

3.4 Models

Your brain is a superb pattern maker. A superior way to learn anything is to make a model of it. Here's a good example. How do you teach people of all ages about brain science? My approach is to use the arms of the students to make a model.

Pretend the palm of your hand is one brain cell. Brain cells are called **neurons**. With a pen, write a big 'N' on the palm of your hand. The palm of your hand will represent the nucleus of one brain cell.

Information comes into your brain from your senses constantly. There are little radar units connected to the top of each brain cell called **dendrites**. Dendrites are always taking in information. Pretend your fingers and thumb are these dendrites. Put a big 'D' on them. Information comes through your dendrites and it's recorded in the nucleus of the neuron. Next, your arm represents the neural telephone line coming out of the bottom of the nucleus. It is called an **axon**. Write a big 'AX' on the side of your arm. The axon ends by splitting into many, many filaments. At the end of each filament there are gaps or spaces. These gaps are called **synapses**. Write an 'S' on your elbow. That's what brain cells look like.

Chemicals are passed through the synapses from one brain cell into the dendrites of another cell and that's how neurons talk to each other.

As each part of the brain cell is written on the arm, its function is explained. Everyone in the class is participating and learning by doing, rather than filling in the blanks on the diagram supplied by the teacher or copying notes off the board. At the end of the lesson students are literally wearing their model home.

Constructing models by hand, drawing mind maps or mentally

visualizing models are powerful ways to engage the brain to learn. Model making champions long-term memory formation.

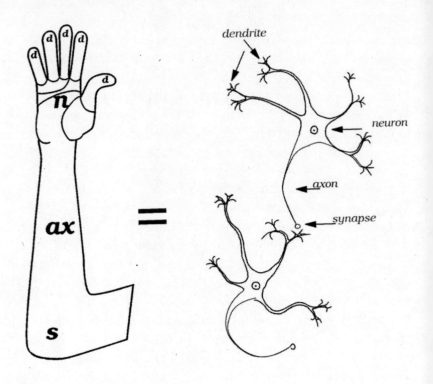

Definitions:

Neuron: the name given to brain cells. All children born today have approximately 100,000,000,000 (100 billion) neurons to start their new lives.

Dendrites: strand-like fibers emanating from the body of the neurons. Dendrites receive information.

Axon: long nerve fiber extending from the neuron. Axons transmit information to other neurons.

Synapse: gap or space at the end of the axon that acts like a junction point. Chemicals pass over the synapses relaying messages.

3.5 Rhymes

Languages are put together by patterns, rhythms and rhymes. In high school, I often taught a key lesson about how brain cells work. How could students possibly remember those brain parts and what they do?

Divide the students into small groups. Assign the challenge of making a rhyming poem, song or rap about brain cells. The goal would be to produce 8 to 10 lines in a certain amount of time. Then each group would perform for the class. Lots of fun and engagement! Here is one of my all time favorites that a Grade 8 class created:

Dendrites are dandy.
Neurons are nifty.
Axons are awesome.
Synapses are super.

Rhymes are powerful memory techniques. If you want to make it stick, rhyme it.

3.6 Music

Does music support learning? Can it help raise intelligence? Accelerated learning techniques say 'YES'. Research says 'YES'. Music has a multitude of practical applications in the classroom and home environment. Music can definitely jumpstart the brain. From personal experience you know that music can influence your heart rate, reduce your stress, make you feel better and give you energy. Music alters brain states. Researchers tell us that music stimulates thinking and creativity, improves contemplation, improves our ability to remember and supports us to learn things in less time.

Does music belong in a Mathematics or English class? Why not? It's outdated thinking to insist that classrooms need to be dead quiet. A totally silent classroom is brain antagonistic. Why not make the learning environment more user-friendly? There are lots of benefits. Music can keep your job interesting and fun and can affect you in many positive ways. Music energizes. Music stimulates the right hemisphere of the brain helping us to be more creative. Music can really reel in those hard to reach kids who find school a hostile alien place.

For best effect, play **Baroque** music in the classroom, at home or in the office. The secret is to play it so quietly that you can barely hear it. Many areas of your brain will be engaged and energized. Baroque music puts you into a positive relaxed state. It's awesome for your brain chemistry. Serotonin and dopamine can be released supporting good positive feelings and therefore a love of learning. Activating positive feelings is an integral part of effective teaching. It is a major part of any teacher's job. Also, this music induces a state of relaxed alertness, a superior brain state. You're actually listening to music that will make you smarter!

The Baroque period of music dates from 1600 to 1750 A.D. The most famous composers are Antonio Vivaldi, George Frederic Handel and Johann Sebastian Bach.

superior music
baroque & classical

not recommended
acid rock, heavy metal

3.7 Metaphors

Relate content to the real world as much as possible. When I'm teaching young elementary school children about brain Science, here's my approach.

I use a tube of toothpaste to show how soft the brain is, a grapefruit to show the size of the brain, an avocado to demonstrate what the texture of the brain is like when you touch it and a sewing needle to explain how small brain cells are. Wow! Thousands of brain neurons can fit on the end of the needle because brain cells are so small.

In high school, I loved to do living metaphors. Senior Social Studies often involved a lot of statistics that were not very exciting. So, I got my students to move with the stats.

Here's a good example. Consider the issue of world hunger. I got all the students in the class to stand up. Everyone in the room represented the entire population of the world. Statistics showed that half of the world's population was malnourished. So, I randomly got half of the students to sit down. No supper for them tonight. The standees did get supper. Great discussions about their personal reactions ensued. Wow! Dry, boring statistics were transformed into a real-life experience. Use metaphors to personalize and gain real perspectives.

> # Learning is best in real life context

3.8 Reciprocal Thinking

Ever noticed how you can lose students or adults during a long 'talking head' speech? If you are a stand and deliver teacher or lecturer, here's a great eye-opener! Lectures turn the brain off. If you want students to pay attention and increase chances of success, then provide them with opportunities to practice reciprocal thinking. Reciprocal thinking is simply sharing. Sharing grows dendrites.

As a rule of thumb, it is most effective to talk no longer than the age of your students. A 13-year-old brain, for example, listens well for about 13 to 15 minutes, then shifts attention elsewhere. Sadly, the teacher keeps on talking. Lectures lack engagement. So, talk for a while and change states by switching activities. It's as simple as getting students to stand up and tell their neighbour what they just heard. Whether in groups of two or four, the discussion only needs to be for a few minutes. Then continue. Alternate between delivering your materials and students sharing the material together. Take this approach several times a lesson. Reciprocal thinking turns the brain on, not off.

3.9 Challenge

For maximum brain growth, challenge students. When the brain gets challenged, it is forced to deviate from old established patterns. Get out of the box. Expand the 2x4 classroom (two covers of the book inside four walls). Give choices. Reduce contrived learning. Variety is the spice of life. Reduce the endless deadly routines that schools impose on students and teachers. Research clearly states that boredom is caused by non-challenging activities. Challenge keeps all of us intellectually active.

Challenge yourself personally. Compete with yourself. Take risks. Break the mold. The brain loves to be challenged at any age. By challenging yourself to upgrade your teaching strategies, you will be growing your own dendrites.

*Cartoonist - Tony Auth

3.10 Optimism

The youth of today are being raised in a very negative, media driven environment. Depression, low self-esteem, hopelessness and unhappiness are visibly evident. Serotonin is lacking. There is a great need to turn these negative brain states around with optimism.

The most positive word in the English language is 'YES'. Saying, speaking, singing, writing 'YES' is the underlying strategy. Make posters with 'YES'. Write 'YES' on your student's work. 'YES' floods the brain with serotonin and paves the way for learning. Cultivate a positive 'YES' attitude in children at an early age and it will alleviate problems later on. There is a never-ending need for the teacher to be optimistic and to teach optimism to students.

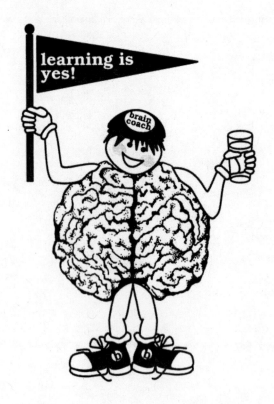

3.11 Prior Knowledge

Has this ever happened to you? You taught a lesson to your class. You had done a lot of preparation and thought that everything went well. Unfortunately the next day, the students had no clue what the lesson was about. Not a clue!

Nothing exists in your brain in isolation. Everything you learn, every skill that you master must be linked into information that is already in your memory bank. New learning will occur easier and faster if it is consistent with old knowledge.

Prior knowledge needs to be engaged. Don't take the old approach of 'open up your book and let's start a new chapter'. Prior knowledge activates the neural networks igniting learning.

There are tremendous benefits for teachers and students. The greater the prior knowledge a student has about a topic, the faster the new material can be integrated. If a topic is introduced to students that is totally new or is completely different from anything they already know, it will be harder for them to master it.

Tips: Before starting some new material find out what the students know about the topic. Try an opening quiz for fun, verbal discussions, advertisement posters, show and tell, website search, guest speaker, conducting an interest inventory or brainstorming online.

3.12 Advertise

"Pay attention!" is a command that you can hear in schools all day long. Teachers need to stop saying that because the truth is that students are always paying attention. They're just not always paying attention to the teacher. It's not possible for students to keep their eyes and ears focused on the teacher every single moment of the day.

A favorite activity of students, when not listening to the teacher, is to just look around. Take advantage of the fact that they will be gazing around the classroom many, many times a lesson. In fact, thousands of times a year. The brain remembers a lot of what it sees and learns from its surroundings. Use peripherals, signs or posters that have simple, meaningful and powerful messages. Advertise. Promote your goals. Get your messages across by making them visual.

3.13 Gestures

Human beings talk to each other using gestures. Gestures supplement and enhance the meaning of what we're trying to say. Children and adolescents imitate our gestures. They are taking a lot of behavioural clues from what is seen, not spoken. The brain pays attention to gestures. Gestures heighten learning.

Only a few years ago neuroscientists discovered **mirror neurons** in the front of the brain. Research reveals that mirror neurons copy what they see. It's one of our primary methods of learning.

When you use gestures, the mirror neurons focus on them. Since getting a student's attention is a big deal, teachers can use mirror neurons to best advantage.

I use a lot of gestures in my workshops. For example, I'm always teaching about the immense benefits of movement. I get my participants to write the word movement in the air with their elbows, with their feet or with their noses while spelling it out loud. Remember, you are continually teaching multiple memory systems and there is memory in muscles.

Information is continually logged in different parts of the brain. The visual part of the brain, the verbal part of the brain and the kinesthetic motor cortex part of the brain are all interconnected and all learn the material at the same time. In other words, the content that you are teaching is being placed in many places in the brain offering more links that can be used later for recall. Don't gestures especially appeal to kinesthetic learners?

Create a treasure trove of usable, fun and practical gestures that you can use over and over again. Keep on inventing new ones too. Learning is all about engagement and gestures engage the brain.

3.14 Memory

How can you help students remember material? The obvious tactic is to teach people about how the memory works. Memory is a living process and is critical to all of us. It is not a thing. Memory is all about the links in your brain: the connections between neurons and the patterns that these connections make.

Memory works best by **repetition**. Reviewing makes memory permanent. Repeat, repeat, repeat! The more you practise and rehearse, the more you can remember.

It is important to note that the brain is not designed to get things the first time. It learns by making mistakes. Parents, caregivers and teachers should make it very clear to students that making mistakes is not bad.

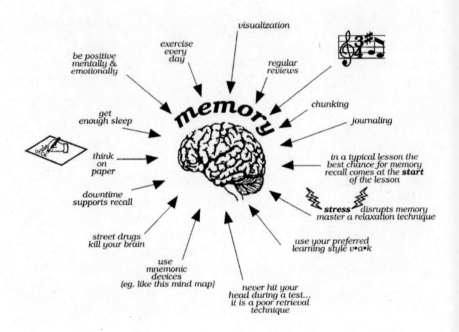

visualization

exercise
every
day

be positive
mentally &
emotionally

regular
reviews

memory

chunking

journaling

get
enough sleep

think
on
paper

in a typical lesson the
best chance for memory
recall comes at the **start**
of the lesson

downtime
supports recall

stress disrupts memory
master a relaxation technique

street drugs
kill your brain

use your preferred
learning style v•a•k

use
mnemonic
devices
(eg. like this mind map)

never hit your
head during a test...
it is a poor retrieval
technique

3.15 Emotional Intelligence

Emotions strongly affect how we either learn or don't learn. Current brain research says that emotions are a cue for the brain to remember. Anything that's followed by emotions, particularly strong emotions, is remembered.

Emotions tell us about setting goals, where to focus and how to set priorities. Emotions allow us to be passionate about learning. Emotional experiences engage the brain and without them retention is unlikely.

Successful parents and teachers engage positive emotions by modeling a love of learning and enthusiasm about their role as educators. Emotional intelligence matters for school achievement, physical health, job success and progress with relationships on all levels.

Conversely, negative emotions block learning. Sarcasm, put-downs, fighting and threats, as well as self-loathing, are all examples of emotional illiteracy. Bullies can be taught peaceful options while introverted kids can be taught self-esteem and social skills.

Pay attention to emotional states. Emphasizing emotional health and well-being is a precursor to success. Honouring the emotional intelligence of our children, our students and fellow workers is a professional and moral responsibility.

4 CHAPTER

Brain Killers

Have you ever hit your computer? Have you ever stomped on your Blackberry? Clobbered your iPad with a hammer? Your computer, Blackberry and iPad are deemed valuable so why wreck them? Why, then, would you want to destroy the most precious thing you own? Your brain!

4.1 Street drugs

Street drugs can do irreparable damage to the human brain. Marijuana, for example, is one of the most common drugs of abuse amongst school-age children, teens and adults. Marijuana cultivates under activity of the frontal lobes in the brain causing undesirable behaviours and motivational problems. The motivational system, unfortunately, can underachieve or even disappear with regular pot smoking. It is not a relaxing, harmless substance. New research from Sweden indicates that marijuana smoking can predispose some teenagers to schizophrenia. Smoking pot often leads to heavier drugs.

Beware of the common label 'recreational drug'. That's an illusion. Street drugs harm the brain. Street drugs change the brain, your personality and your future.

4.2 Alcohol

Alcohol is the most commonly used lethal drug. There is well-established evidence outlining the harmful effects of alcohol on the brain. Fetal alcohol syndrome and fetal alcohol effect cause huge developmental and learning delays in children often robbing them of a successful future. Alcohol related abuse creates challenges for teachers, parents, schools and society as a whole. Problems can be prevented through early education and intervention.

Modern brain-imaging techniques provide powerful teaching and awareness tools for everyone. Brain imaging is changing the world in which we live. What kind of brain do you want? I highly recommend you view the brain scans available at www.mindworkspress.com (SPECT Atlas). My audiences are continually shocked when they see the difference between beautiful, healthy brains and those destroyed by drugs and alcohol. You abuse, you lose.

4.3 Television

In today's world, electronic activities are usurping traditional activities. Human beings learn best when they are face-to-face with other people. Electronic devices cannot replace the day-to-day social interaction that is critical for healthy development.

The American Academy of Pediatrics recommends no television viewing for children until they've had their second birthday.

Television viewing needs to be monitored. Watching television should be a treat rather than an escape. Excessive television viewing downshifts your brain because of the bombardment from constantly changing streams of pictures, words and disconnected images.

The best advice for teachers, parents and caregivers is to repeatedly ask the following question. Will this program support the children's education? Yes or no? Choose programs that support rather than belittle. Choose programs that build the neural networks rather than overload and confuse the brain. There are endless better alternatives to watching TV.

Excessive television viewing causes many troubling problems. Abuse, overuse or escape contribute to concerns such as:

- electronic sedation
- mental passivity
- less verbal interaction
- poor social skills
- reduced motor skills
- loss of language
- short attention spans
- delayed vision
- lost opportunities
- no imagination
- no creativity
- a disadvantaged brain

CAUTION:
CHILDREN NOT AT PLAY.

4.4 Video games

Video games work on the pleasure centers of the brain. Video games can be highly addictive. Modest benefits are strongly outweighed by the drawbacks. Video games do not really work the brain unless they are educationally oriented. Critics of video games state that video games dumb you down. No dialogue is taking place between real people. Video games and computer games slow down the progress of brain development for children, teens and people of all ages.

Warning: Violent electronic games are hazardous to mental health and contribute to aggressive, antisocial behavior. Media violence inspires real violence.

4.5 Sleep deprivation

Why are students of all ages so tired these days? Children, teenagers and their parents don't seem to be getting enough sleep. How much sleep do we need? The average person sleeps about eight hours in a night. Children and teenagers need much more.

The brain is only capable of being awake and alert for 16 hours a day. After that, efficiency is compromised. Extended wakefulness causes neurons to malfunction. Without sleep, the brain can't operate efficiently causing problems of poor grades at school, inability to focus, irritability and a host of other undesirable effects.

Memories are formed during sleep. Useless and irrelevant information is dumped while important information is filed. Lack of sleep means storage and repair work can't get done and we forget more easily. Lack of sleep means we won't get optimal brain performance the next day. Sleep is especially critical for students during exam times.

Educating children, parents and teachers about the importance of sleep is just as significant as educating them about personal hygiene, nutrition or alcohol abuse. Sleep is not a waste of time. It is an investment and is critical for health and well-being.

A well-rested brain is crucial. If you want to be mentally sharp and do well in school then get a good night's sleep. Your perpetually learning brain is a major player in your life. Give it what it needs.

Sleep deprivation is becoming a most common brain impairment

4.6 Concussions

Concussions are brain injuries. Protect your brain. Invest in high quality helmets and equipment. Neuroscience is changing the way we live forever. With the huge interest in brain concussions these days, parents need to make wise decisions. Are you going to place your children into a sport or activity in which one punch, blow or kick can cause permanent brain damage? Sports like hockey, football and boxing are serious threats to brain health. Why put your loved ones there?

The most valuable thing you own, your little 3 pound brain, is as soft as tofu

Special Brains

More and more students have learning disorders or behaviour issues. These students provide the biggest and most frustrating challenges for teachers. Here are some totally practical ways to help those with Attention Disorders, Oppositional Disorders and Learned Helplessness. Being able to cope and work with special brains will make a dramatic improvement in the classroom for these students, their classmates and you.

There are many forces that stop the brain from learning. Students of all ages have been diagnosed with ADD, ADHD, oppositional disorder, learning delays of all kinds, fetal alcohol syndrome, fetal alcohol effect, various conduct disorders, depression, stress, autism, brain injuries, dyslexia, sensory integration disorders, auditory processing deficits, drug abuse disorders, alcohol abuse disorders and many more.

These challenges are with us in every classroom. Ignoring them will not bring success. Neither will hoping that these issues just disappear one day. The numbers will definitely increase. There is a need for teachers, parents and caregivers to know more about how to help.

5.1 Learned Helplessness

Ever have children or students who have the attitude of "who cares", "why bother" or "if I pass this test or I fail this test, it doesn't matter". Learned helplessness appears as inertia, apathy, passiveness or even withdrawal. Learned helplessness is a serious condition in which students feel powerless to control their own fate. They have learned to be unmotivated. Generally speaking they are not lazy nor do they need punishment. They have learned to be helpless. If they have learned to be helpless, then they can unlearn it.

Learned helplessness is a real challenge to deal with in the classroom because these students can easily pollute the rest of the class. I personally found them to be the most challenging of all the special brain students to work with. They can take a lot of time and energy unless you have your strategies in place.

Top strategies:

1. Support these students with optimism, not punishment. Get them to say the word 'YES' as much as possible to re-wire their attitudes and their brain.

2. Give lots of choices. Provide them with some measure of control of their learning in school. Jobs, responsibilities and duties are needed. Any opportunity to excel in leadership roles needs to be pursued. Involving students in drama productions provides a great opportunity. Social settings offer lots of opportunities in which other people need to rely on them.

3. Encourage movement and exercise. Get them out of their inert, slouching, slothful postures in the desk and get them up dancing, singing, playing sports or any other physical challenge that provides some sort of risk-taking activity.

4. This final tip is totally magic. I had a colourful poster above my desk that said, 'The ignition key needs to be turned ____.'. The answer of course is 'ON'. This was a powerful tool for making students instantly aware of their present non-learning brain state and the need for correction.

5.2 Oppositional Disorder (OPD)

OPD students are very argumentative. Often times the only word they use is 'NO'. Unfortunately, they can be very confrontational and defiant. They also can unleash temper tantrums, upsetting others.

What is wrong? Oppositional disorder individuals have a stuck brain. They can't switch gears or change brain states. The same sorts of conflicts are continually repeated. Arguing or butting heads with oppositional students does not work. No one wins. It can be stressful for everyone. Here are some survival strategies that you can implement to support them to learn and gain success instead of frustration and confrontation.

Top strategies:

1. Be prepared. Know exactly what you're going to do when you get into an oppositional situation. Know exactly what you're

going to say. Have your patented responses ready.

2. Avoid arguing with OPD children and students. Instead of ultimatums, give choices. Choices change brain states giving you the opportunity to get oppositional students unstuck.

3. Posturing is important. When addressing an oppositional student, sit beside him or her. Avoid standing in front of them with an aggressive stance such as folded arms or pointed fingers.

4. Use humour, a lot.

5. Journal writing and drawing encourage positive expression. I was amazed at how many times I could diffuse very angry, upset oppositional students by simply pulling out the pencil crayon box and encouraging them to colour a Mandala. Colouring calms the brain and produces more relaxing brain frequencies. Don't forget relaxed alertness is a basic principle for engaging the RAS.

6. Get support and create a behaviour management plan. Don't take OPD personally as it's not about you. I can't count the number of times in my career that I have seen teachers repeatedly get into arguments and conflicts with OPD students. I could almost predict it. You can't win by arguing. Remember, it's not about you.

5.3 Attention-Deficit Disorders (ADD, ADHD)

Attention Deficit Disorder and Attention Deficit Hyperactive Disorder are the most commonly diagnosed behavioural disorders.

The problem lies with the frontal lobes. Here are typical challenges and behaviours with attention deficit disorder students: out of sync with time, unable to attend to the future, very disorganized, lack patience, can't sit still, always moving and fidgeting, blurting out answers in class and having short-term memory issues.

Top strategies:

1. **Demystify.** My approach was always to teach students what was going on in their brain regardless of their grade or subject. I would explain to them that their attention difficulties were all about their 'Captain'.

ADD students bounce around, wiggle and squirm to get their 'Captain on deck'. It's a natural reaction. If they need to have their thinking 'Captain' working for them, then they have to move to engage it.

Through movement, the students were doing exactly what was needed to be done. So, knowing this, whenever they were unable to focus, sit still or pay attention, I would purposefully get them up and moving. For example: go to the library to get the newspaper, go for a jog around school, staple papers, sort papers, sharpen pencils, etc. By doing this, the 'Captain' became engaged because their brain state changed after they had moved.

Demystifying makes sense. Teach and empower students about what exactly is going on. Make it simple for them. Get them to ask for brain breaks, energizers or state changes if they are really losing it. Brain-based learning is all about supporting students to learn how to manage their own states and empower themselves.

2. Signals. Since impulsivity is a major issue, teach students the value of waiting. Add signals and gestures to your teaching toolbox.

3. Help with **organization** is a must. ADD brains are often

very disorganized. They have trouble completing assignments and getting things done on time. Planner books, diaries and calendars provide excellent support.

Special Brain students can take up a lot of your time, energy and patience. My time honoured advice for teachers and parents would be:

✓ never give up on a child or a student
✓ always show that you care
✓ believe that everyone can learn
✓ hope is a powerful motivator

6
CHAPTER

The Child's Brain

The way we raise our children has the greatest possible consequences. The better the brain that children have, the better decisions children will be able to make. The better the decisions children can make, the better actions they will be able to perform. The better actions they undertake, the better results they will get throughout their entire life. The greater the brain, the greater the potential! Is it possible to grow a child's brain? DEFINITELY YES!!

It wasn't long ago that society viewed the child's brain as a static and unchanging organ. Nothing could be farther from the truth. Parents, caregivers and teachers can certainly help create a great brain for children. The brain undergoes dramatic and constant transformations from birth. The most important time in a person's entire life is in early childhood.

The child's brain is a highly dynamic organ that feeds on stimulation. The brain responds by growing forests of neural connections, dendrites and synapses, preparing the way for cognitive development. The highly plastic, constantly changing human brain has a limitless potential.

Children are born with literally billions and billions of neurons. These neurons must learn how to talk and communicate with each other by forming vital connections. The neural pathways that they form provide the foundations for learning, hearing, vision, language, thinking and feeling.

What is the determining factor? Is it nature or is it nurture? Nature is our genetic inheritance. Nurture is about our life experiences.

Imagine a 10 point scale: 3 to 4 points would be contributed from Mother Nature while nurturing would supply 6 to 7 points. We have a great deal to say about how genes behave and how they develop. Genes determine the number and quality of brain cells that you're born with but environmental influences control the turning on and off of those genes.

Children do not arrive with a user's manual. The environment plays a huge role in learning, intelligence and future academic success in life. The most effective environments would include: mental stimulation, correct food and nutrients, lots of physical activity, emotional security and the experience of feeling loved by parents. Great brains are made.

Sadly, negative environments limit the children's chances of achieving their full potential. Poor diets, lack of mental stimulation and stressful households retard the chances of success in life from the very beginning.

How do you grow a child's brain? What makes the brain more efficient, stronger, faster and smarter? The following powerful lifestyle choices and teaching strategies provide the right stimulation in early childhood giving children the best opportunities to perform and excel from diapers to the classroom.

6.1 Nurturing

To realize the fullest potential of the brain and body, children must be reared in sheltered and nurturing environments. How children are nurtured as infants and youngsters strongly influences the kind of people they are going to grow up to be. The child's brain is hardwired by empathy, caring, compassion and love. Contact through breast-feeding, emotional nurturing and being held in the arms of parents and caregivers are all part of nature's design. These practices support the enrichment of the brain and translate into positive developmental advantages.

Physical and emotional closeness to children needs to be encouraged. A solid foundation of bonding and connecting with parents and siblings will bring forth healthy, happy, peaceful and joyful human beings. The first step toward building a great brain is made by conscious nurturing parents.

6.2 Safety

It's difficult to learn if you don't feel safe. Children raised in stress-free environments have the greatest potential. The brain's principal task is to survive in order to keep learning. It's not possible to learn if the flight or fight response is constantly on or the brain is full of stress chemicals. Eliminate sarcasm, putdowns, bullying, threats and fear because they disrupt learning.

6.3 Time in Nature

More and more research shows that contact with nature is extremely important for children. Time in nature is just as important as adequate sleep and good nutrition. Outdoor play means increased physical activity and fitness that increases the children's ability to focus and stay on task. Playing outdoors is critical and needed for healthy development of the child's brain, body and mind. Nature provides healing, harmony and balance.

Children need to draw connections between what they're learning in school and in the world around them. How can we expect future generations to care for the earth if they had no connection with it? Avoid nature-deficit disorder. Early childhood educators, caregivers and parents have to have an enlightened look at their responsibilities in connecting young children to the natural world.

6.4 Ask Questions

Questions turn on the Reticular Activating System of the brain. Do you want children to pay attention to you? If you want to tell them something really important, do it by asking them a question.

Questions evoke discussions and build problem-solving skills. Questions generate new ideas. Did you know that students struggling academically rarely ask questions in class? It's really significant for children, who are low achievers in school, to cultivate a habit of asking a lot of questions. Encourage all children to do so.

So parents, here is an awesome brain compatible parenting strategy. How many times have parents asked their kids the classic question of the ages "What did you learn in school today?". And how many times did you get the standard answer "Nothing!". Unfortunately, this goes on year after year, grade after grade. Parents ask the same question and children respond with the same answer "Nothing!". Wrong approach.

If you want to be a superstar parent, don't ask that brain-dead question anymore. Here's a much better approach. Say to them "**What questions did you ask in school today?**". This demonstrates very clearly to the children that you are interested in what's going on in their life. Questions are far more important than information. Questions are what learning and thinking are really all about. Encourage and support your kids to ask tons of questions every day, at home and at school. That's how scholars are made. Put your children on track to academic success from the very start.

6.5 Storytelling

Everyone loves stories because we are all hard-wired by nature for listening to stories from the moment we are born. Children really love to listen to stories. Listening to stories rich in imagery and expressive language starts the brain off on the right foot. Stories for children stimulate the right hemisphere of their brain helping them to relax and process all the new ideas and words they are hearing. Stories hook learners, igniting young imaginations. Storytelling literally lights up the whole brain. Tell stories to your children absolutely every single day. Get them to tell you stories too. The development of language requires daily practice in conversation.

6.6 Reading

Reading grows dendrites. Reading is the best channel in town. Right from the moment children are born, make reading stories an integral part of the daily routine.

Read stories while children are sitting on your lap. Get them to turn the pages. Model the appropriate way to hold and read a book and they will be on their way. Let them collect books and develop their own library as they grow up. Also, don't forget the public library. Libraries are cost free and available to everyone.

Why read? When children learn to speak English, Spanish, French or any other language, they have to become familiar with the basic sounds of **phonemes**. Phonemes are what we use to make words. Children's brains are wired for speech much earlier than they are wired for reading. That's why kids learn to talk first before they can read. Their future decision-making skills, problem-solving skills and development depends on their understanding of language. There's no substitute for daily language reinforcement by parents, caregivers and siblings. Even if you're very busy and you don't have much time, definitely squeeze in a minute or two to read to your children. Reading fosters language and language is a measure of intelligence.

6.7 Imagination

Youngsters have fantastic active imaginations. The preschool years offer major opportunities for encouraging inventiveness. Support imaginary friendships and pretend playmates that the children have. There is nothing wrong with children having their own private conversation.

When a young child picks up a stone and pretends it's a rocket ship, play the game with them. An ordinary stick could be a light saber or a magic wand or a spyglass transporting the child into a wonderful world of make believe. Encourage imagination by avoiding judgments and criticisms.

Imaginative play is how children learn, paving the way for abstract thinking. A well developed imagination is essential for advanced brain development. Imaginative play and daydreaming promote the child's intellect setting the stage for future academic success.

One of my biggest challenges in high school for years was helping students getting started on a writing assignment. Whether it was a short paragraph or an essay, it was always the same issue. They couldn't get started. They couldn't even choose what to write about. Why? No imagination. If you cannot imagine something, then you have a lot of trouble writing about it.

> ## "Imagination is more powerful than knowledge."
> Albert Enstein

6.8 Creativity

All human beings are inherently creative. Give kids time and space to create. They will naturally entertain themselves without adult supervision. Encourage children to be creative on all levels. Why limit them to the standard and conventional? Create potentials. Explore the world.

Let children come up with new ideas and new ways of doing things. Teach children using analogies and metaphors. Let them make decisions and take risks. Raise them to enjoy thinking and working independently as well as with other children of all ages. A creative child is a whole brain in action. That exploring, mobile, chattering preschooler has a supercharged brain full of great creative potential.

6.9 Play for Fun

Play is the essence of life. Nature intended children to play. Play establishes and stimulates multiple neural pathways all over the brain for learning, experiencing and relating to life. Playing builds endless connections that promote intelligence and emotional stability. Play is a hardwired biological drive.

Have you noticed how young children have a compulsion to play? Children love to play. Play is essential for growth and development. Play is the natural and genuine way the brain learns best.

Play helps children to function as human beings with thoughts, feelings and actions maturing together in a coordinated way. Skills learned in playing are transferred to the real world. Playing supports and produces an anxiety-free brain that can learn at an astonishing rate. Encourage children to play. Support children to play. Learn to play at learning. Children learn lifelong skills through physical play.

Athletes, actors and artists talk about being "in the flow" or " in the zone". When you are "in the zone", you are totally and completely at ease with what is happening. This is when wonderful things can be created, extraordinary masterpieces can materialize and great results can occur. When children are playing, they are "in the zone".

The magical state of playing means children are:

✓ being totally present
✓ paying attention
✓ trusting in the moment
✓ lacking fear
✓ enjoying life

When children are playing, the brain is in a homeostatic state. This is a condition in which feelings, thoughts and actions are balanced and coordinated. Then wonderful things happen:

✓ errors don't exist
✓ time is not a factor
✓ stress is reduced
✓ the brain is anxiety free
✓ children can investigate the unknown safely
✓ children are open to creative exploration
✓ children are open to creative expression
✓ children are using their active imagination
✓ children are learning without conflict
✓ children are not preoccupied with success or failure
✓ children are rehearsing for adult life

In the early formative years, play is almost synonymous with life. Play is second only to being protected, loved and nurtured. What is the basic ingredient for physical intellectual, social and emotional growth? Play!

6.10 Experience

Who are the architects of the child's brain? The parents are. Parents will decide either consciously or unconsciously what kind of brain the child will ultimately have. It's up to the parents to develop the best brain possible. There are endless opportunities to do so. Find a few minutes every day to play with your child, read to your child and talk to your child. Provide rich home environments in which children can engage in safe, imaginative play. Don't forget, the child's abilities are hardwired during these early years. The more the brain does, the more it is intellectually capable of doing.

Every child has a lifelong growing potential if he or she gets lots of experience. The types of experience that children have determine how the brain will grow. Rich experiences grow a rich brain. Rich experiences drive the development of the brain. Is your family environment, your daycare environment or your school environment brain compatible?

Dr. Marian Diamond writes in 'Magic Trees of the Mind':

"The brain, with its complex architecture and limitless potential, is a highly plastic, changing entity that is powerfully shaped by experiences in childhood and throughout life."

7
CHAPTER

The Teenage Brain

What goes on in the teenage brain? Here are some great insights into the mysterious teenage brain, helping to bridge the gap between research and practical advice for parents, teachers and society in general. These 10 strategies can help effectively reach and teach adolescents, leading them to academic success.

"At your age, Tommy, a boy's body goes through changes that are not always easy to understand."

The teenage brain is a work in progress. Huge changes are occurring. Have you ever wondered why teenagers do the wacky things they do? What is going on inside the teenage brain that accounts for their emotional outbursts, reckless rule breaking, weird and sometimes, dangerous behaviour?

It's biological turmoil! The adolescent brain is pruning away millions and millions of neural connections. Reconstructing, reconnecting and reshaping are going on constantly. A new brain is being built.

The brain develops in stages from back to front. The last part of the brain to be seasoned to its full adult dimensions is the 'Captain' or the prefrontal cortex. Remember, this is the home of your executive functions such as making judgments, dealing with impulses, higher level thinking, decision making, etc. It is this thinking part of the brain that is the last part to fully mature.

For parents and caregivers, it is vital to provide structure and guidance to apply the wise virtues of patience and love. Teenagers need their parents and guardians. They need to live in a family atmosphere. Spend quality time with them. Be interested in their lives. Talk and listen to them. Do things with them. Remember, though, that teenagers also need quiet alone time as a balance to their busy world.

It is a great time in the teenager's life to build a great brain or waste its potential. Teenagers have the opportunity to influence the development of their own brains through the activities and experiences they choose to take part in.

7.1 The Social Teenage Brain

If you ask teenagers what is the most important thing in the world for them, they will invariably say my 'friends'. Teenagers are extremely social. Relationships with their friends are what life is all about. Social interaction is an essential component of brain compatible teaching and learning.

Social interaction is a key part of supporting teenagers to learn and grow. If we want to engage them in the learning process then they need to work in teams, groups, with buddies, in co-op learning experiences or as peer tutors. Their future depends upon being able to actively listen to each other, to work in groups, to create and solve problems together. That is a challenge because a lot of technology available today tends to put teenagers in isolation.

Humans are social creatures and social conditions influence and change the brain. It's up to the teacher and parents to orchestrate positive social conditions. Social Neuroscientists tell us that humans have evolved in this world because of our connections with other people. Our social brain is a major player in understanding why we have survived thousands of years of history.

> **The teenage brain excels in music, sports, art, visual arts, drama, role-playing, acting, dancing and singing**

7.2 The Emotional Teenage Brain

Teenagers process emotions differently than adults do. Adults rely on their frontal lobes to help deal with their emotions and emotional reactions. Adolescents, on the other hand, rely heavily on the amygdala. The amygdala is a small almond shaped organ in the brain that operates our fear switch. It activates in reaction to threats and triggers the fight, flight or freeze response. The amygdala is the decision maker that helps to explain emotional and impulsive behaviour. The teenage brain reacts emotionally not logically because the prefrontal cortex is not yet mature. Teenagers, sometimes, can't make good smart emotional decisions or they misread emotional signals because they're depending on the amygdala. That makes long-term thinking tough.

Teachers and parents need to understand that teenagers, at times, can be highly emotional, easily excitable and very passionate youths.

7.3 Nutrition

Since the brain's major source of nutrition is oxygen, teenagers need to move. Everyday! Neuroscientific research emphatically states how absolutely necessary physical movement and aerobic exercise are for achieving optimal brain functioning, enhancing learning and enjoying good health. The bottom line is raise teenagers in motion. Exercise programs are not optional, they are mandatory. A sedentary lifestyle is lunacy for a teenager. The more exercise they get, the healthier their brain will be making it easier to learn.

When young children become teenagers, bump up nutrition. Feed the teenage brain a diet of nutritious foods. Avoid junk foods. Junk foods make brain cells rigid and inefficient. Provide good healthy meals as malnourished brains have difficulty learning. Don't forget, the key meal of the day is breakfast.

Make sure protein is on the breakfast menu because you need protein to make neurotransmitters. In their packsacks, teenagers need to have a water bottle, nutritious snacks and a good lunch as they head out the door for school. Finally, eat dinner together as a family. If we don't feed the teenage brain what it needs most, how is it supposed to develop and mature into a great brain?

7.4 Organization

The teenage brain can be very disorganized at times. Provide help with planner books, diaries, calendars, and plenty of support. For years I would tell students, you may not like your planner book but your brain does so that's why you are required to use it everyday in my class.

Have a big calendar at home in which all family members write on their appointments, due dates for school projects, field trips, practices, etc. That way everybody can see the big picture. This helps defuse stress and keeps teenagers on track. The best place to have this calendar is on the fridge door! ADD students especially need organizational support.

7.5 Feedback

Feedback is a huge issue. Frequent feedback keeps learners motivated. It is in line with how the brain learns best naturally. The best feedback is immediate, positive and continuous. Teenagers thrive on feedback because it reduces uncertainty and stress. Feedback is important so that they can correct their mistakes and ask for help if they don't understand. Also, there is a need to find out how well they did or if there is a need for improvement. It keeps them going in the right direction and doing their best. Feedback is more than quizzes, unit tests or final exams. It's about how we're doing as a person. If it comes from the teenagers themselves, that is even better.

Foster feedback in your school and home environment on a daily basis. Feedback is important to all players in our society including parents, students, teachers and especially vulnerable, immature teenagers.

Tips: Types of feedback include: peer review, teacher comments, written comments, self-review, discussions, previews or corrections. Daily feedback is mandatory for success.

The brain thrives on feedback for growth, learning and survival

---

7.6 Brain Smarts

Brain smart teenagers. A brain smart teenager knows his or her own personal learning style. They fully understand that the brain grows by learning. Brain smart students know how their brain functions, thrives and works well for them. Brain smart students believe in their brain. They know how to manage their own brain states. Their success in life depends on a well developed brain and they know it. It's the most valuable thing they own so they invest in it. The brain is treated with dignity and respect.

Proper nutrition, adequate sleep, daily exercise, downtime plus a super positive, optimistic attitude toward learning build a great brain. These will empower teenagers to become great thinkers.

Brain smart students also know that education and learning are important. Schools are important. Success in school means success in life. The more education you have, the more your life can improve, increasing your potentials. Be brain smart and learn how use it before you lose it.

Top Tip: What you learn in school is not as important as how you learn it. Learning <u>how</u> to study subjects is far more valuable than the material in the course. Study skills are priceless life skills.

7.7 Role Models

Teenagers are constantly looking for meaningful and relevant role models. They're looking for someone to copy, someone to emulate. Inspiration comes from the lives of others motivating teenagers to achieve their fullest potential. Parents and teachers are the closest adults. Be a good model for your teens. In reality, they are learning more about who you are as a person than what you are teaching them.

7.8 Hands-On Activities

Tactile learning is the superior way of learning. We make our best neural connections by actually doing things. When you physically grab, clutch, grip, lift, carry, fix, break or toss something your best memories are formed. These experiences sculpt the strongest pathways in your brain. It's easiest to remember something while you are actually doing it.

Schools are set up to favour visual learners. Auditory learners are tolerated. Unfortunately, kinesthetic learners are often discouraged or even punished. Hands-on activities are a great asset for all students, especially the kinesthetic ones. Brain-based learning honours all three learning styles.

7.9 Novelty

Teenagers crave novelty. The teenage brain loves novelty and seeks it. The brain focuses on new and unfamiliar things, an ancient inherited trait from our ancestors. Novelty stimulates production of dopamine, our all-time feeling good neurotransmitter. That's why teenagers often do crazy and unpredictable things. Novelty supplies dopamine and teenagers love dopamine.

Novelty keeps your brain fully functioning and alive. Dull, endlessly boring, predictable routine shuts off the brain. High schools often dish out this type of brain dead experience. For teenagers it is the same old, same old, same old. Ideally, there needs to be a balance between regular routine and novelty. Break the mold. Escape from the lethargy of custom. Bored, tuned out teenagers are not getting enough stimulation. Teenagers crave novelty, not drill and kill.

7.10 Episodes

Since dynamic growth is happening in the teenage brain all the time, teenagers naturally love novelty and challenge. Traditional teaching relies heavily on learning and mastering of endless, unconnected, isolated information bits. The brain does not like isolated information because it needs to connect with other things it already knows. This causes big-time boredom in the teenage brain. Over time this turns them off producing comments like "School sucks." or "School is boring.". Those comments are often justified.

The strongest and most meaningful memories are the experiences that you have had. These experiences are recorded as episodic memories. Using episodic memory is a great way to teach and engage teenagers. They love getting outside the box. Teenagers crave anything different, weird, crazy, funny, spontaneous, stupid, irrational, etc. Unique learning experiences are critical for the evolving teenage brain. Episodes engage the teenage brain. Episodes ignite a love of learning. Create new ones everyday.

Teenagers need to leave every class with experiences not notes

8
CHAPTER

The Biggest Challenge Ahead

Education is all about progressive change

The students of today have much different brains than students of previous years. As well, the student brain is often different from the teacher's brain. New environments have brought new kids to schools. What is shaping the brains of today? The changes are monumental.

You're probably familiar with junk food diets, caffeine, sugar loaded pop, drug use, the dramatic shifts in family patterns, television and video game influences. Today's students are "digital" which means their brains have been wired by electronics. They have been exposed to electronic toys since birth. Digital brains thrive on instant gratification and function in a virtual world that offers a continuous bombardment of information bytes. Texting, Facebook, social networking sites, games, anytime anywhere technology is their world.

This presents great challenges in the classroom. Students are less verbal and less linguistic. They are more visually oriented. Interest is definitely with graphics before text. Attention spans are shorter. Chronic partial attention issues can be found in all grades. Students are getting harder to teach.

The majority of students are right-brained. So? Our time honoured, traditional teaching techniques are not designed for right brain learners. School systems are predominately left brain. The old teaching techniques are not leading to achievement levels that have come to be expected in the past.

Education is really all about progressive change. If students today have different brains, who needs to change? Embracing differentiated instructional strategies is not an option, it is mandatory for the survival of all levels of education.

Brain-based learning provides a new focus for schools and at home. The emphasis needs to be on how to engage the brain and keep it engaged.

Teachers, don't get caught frozen in time. You teach brains every single day. Brain-based learning strategies turn on the student brain. Your students will love you for promoting a love of learning not just cramming for the next test. They'll show up every day ready and willing to learn. Isn't it socially imperative that schools focus on developing the learner's brain? Teaching the way the brain learns best naturally is a critical educational reform that has to be initiated.

If you want to help children and students to learn in today's world, then you need to begin with their brain!

Parent Tips

✪ The brain has everything to do with learning. Parents are literally the architects of the child's brain. Applying brain-based learning principles will develop a superior, brain friendly home learning environment.

✪ SAFETY FIRST. Children need to be raised in a loving and supportive environment. Feeling safe means the brain produces positive brain chemicals allowing neurons to communicate with each other and grow. Keep the brain upshifted.

✪ Teach children how the brain learns. Motivate them to become life long learners.

✪ Do more than "tell" children. The brain learns best through MODELING.

✪ Time is needed to develop the prefrontal cortex. Don't push.

✪ MOVEMENT, EXERCISE AND FREE PLAY grow the best brain.

✪ Use all of the SENSES. Provide lots of multi sensory experiences to produce multiple pathways in the brain.

✪ Success means being able to control EMOTIONS rather than being controlled by them.

✪ STRESS can delay learning. Learn and practise stress releasing activities.

✪ DOWNTIME is needed daily. Learning occurs through internal processing.

- ❂ Meet the BIOLOGICAL needs of the brain. Good nutrition, water, sleep and exercise provide the required raw materials.

- ❂ An attitude of GRATITUDE sets the stage for life long learning.

- ❂ CREATIVITY needs to be encouraged at every age. It is essential to our nature as human beings.

- ❂ Every day is a great day to learn something.

- ❂ COMMON SENSE dictates how the brain learns best. Use it.

Learning is magic when you have the knowledge

CHECKLIST

Your Magical Brain
How The Brain Learns Best

- ✓ MOVEMENT
- ✓ RECIPROCAL THINKING
- ✓ EPISODES
- ✓ NOVELTY
- ✓ DOWNTIME
- ✓ FEEDBACK
- ✓ BRAIN STATES
- ✓ STORY TELLING
- ✓ MODELS
- ✓ POSITIVE EMOTIONS
- ✓ MUSIC
- ✓ ORGANIZATION
- ✓ PRIOR KNOWLEDGE
- ✓ TIME IN NATURE
- ✓ LEARNING STYLES
- ✓ SAFETY
- ✓ RITUALS
- ✓ CHALLENGE
- ✓ PLAY FOR FUN
- ✓ HUMOUR
- ✓ OPTIMISM
- ✓ OXYGEN
- ✓ WATER
- ✓ HEALTHY DIET
- ✓ RHYMES
- ✓ UPSHIFTING
- ✓ EXPERIENCE
- ✓ READING
- ✓ CARING
- ✓ REPETITION

Bibliography

Amen, Daniel. (1999). Change Your Brain Change Your Life, A Berkley Book.

Amen, Daniel. (2003). Images Of Human Behavior: A Brain Spect Atlas, The Amen Clinic.

Anaka, Gary. (2009). Brain Wellness the Secrets for Longevity, Portal Press.

Clavier, Ron. (2005). Teen Brain, Teen Mind: What Parents Need to Know to Survive the Adolescent Years, Ontario Arts Council.

Campbell, Don. (2001). The Mozart Effect, Quill Publishers.

Corbin, Barry. (2008). Unleashing The Potential of the Teenage Brain: 10 Powerful Ideas, Corwin Press.

Dennison, Paul. (1989). Brain Gym: The Teacher's Edition Revised, The Educational Kinesiology Foundation.

Diamond, Marian & Hopson, Janet. (1998). Magic Trees of the Mind, Penguin Group.

Erlauer, Laura. (2003). The Brain-Compatible Classroom: Using What We Know About Learning To Improve Teaching, ASCD.

Evanski, Jerry. (2004). Classroom Activators: 64 Novel Ways to Energize Learners, Corwin Press.

Feinstein, Sheryl. (2009). Secrets Of The Teenage Brain, Corwin Press.

Goleman, Daniel. (1995). Emotional Intelligence, Bantam Books.

Gregory, Gayle and Chapman, Carolyn. (2007). Differentiated Instructions Strategies: One Size Doesn't Fit All, Corwin Press.

Hannaford, Carla. (1995). Smart Moves: Why Learning Is Not All In Your Head, Great Ocean Publishers.

Healy, Jane. (1994). Your Child's Growing Mind: A Practical Guide to Brain Development and Learning From Birth to Adolescence, Double Day.

Healy, Jane. (1990). Endangered Minds: Why Children Don't

Think and What We Can Do About It, Simon and
Schuster.

Jensen, Eric. (2009). Super Teaching, Corwin Press.

Jensen, Eric. (2008). Brain-Based Learning, Corwin Press.

Jensen, Eric. (2004). Different Brains, Different Learners:
How To Reach The Hard To Reach, Corwin Press.

Jensen, Eric. (2003). Tools For Engagement, Corwin Press.

Kaufeldt, Martha. (2010). Begin With The Brain, Corwin
Press.

Miller, Jeffrey. (2009). Understanding and Engaging
Adolescents, Corwin Press.

Nash, Ron. (2009). The Active Classroom: Practical
Strategies for Involving Students in the Learning
Process, Corwin Press.

Perlmutter, David. (2006). Raise A Smarter Child By
Kindergarten, Morgan Road Books.

Politano, Colleen and Paquin, Joy. (2000). Brain-Based
Learning With Class, Portage & Main Press.

Raleigh, Philip. (2007). Engaging 'Tweens and Teens, Corwin
Press.

Small, Gary. (2008). i Brain: Surviving the Technological
Alteration of the Modern Mind, Harper Collins.

Sousa, David. (2005). How The Brain Learns, Harper
Collins.

Sprenger, Marilee. (2008). The Developing Brain, Birth To
Age 8, Corwin Press.

Summerford, Cathie. (2009). Action-Packed Classrooms,
Corwin Press.

Sylwester, Robert. (2010). A Child's Brain: The Need for
Nurture, Corwin Press.

Sylwester, Robert. (2007). The Adolescent Brain: Reaching
for Autonomy, Corwin Press.

Tate, Marcia. (2010). Worksheets Don't Grow Dendrites,
Corwin Press.

Wolfe, Pat. (2010). Brain Matters, Translating Research into
Classroom Practise, ASCD.

General Reference

Blaylock, Russell. (1997). Excitotoxins – The Taste that Kills, Health Press.

Doidge, Norman. (2007). The Brain That Changes Itself, Penguin Books.

Howard, Pierce. (2006). The Owner's Manual for the Brain, Bard Press.

Khalsa, Dharma Singh. (1997). Brain Longevity, Warner Books.

Perlmutter, David. (2004). The Better Brain Book, Riverhead Books.

Pratt, Steven and Matthews, Kathy. (2004). Superfoods RX: Fourteen Foods That Will Change Your Life, Harper Collins.

Website Suggestions
Information About The Brain

Latest research?
> www.sfn.org
> www.sciencedaily.com
> www.dana.com

Learning?
> www.scientificamerican.com

Fun?
> www.brain.com

Free Resources

> Neuroscience for Kids Newsletter
> http://faculty.washington.edu/chudler/newslet.html
> **Excellent resource for children and teens of all ages**

Public Broadcasting Service Teacher Source
http://www.pbs.org
Great resource for teachers regarding the brain

Brain Imaging

SPECT Atlas
www.mindworkspress.com
Excellent brain scans

Whole Brain Atlas
http://www.med.harvard.edu/AANLIB/home.html

About The Author

 Gary Anaka has over 32 years of teaching experience in the classroom as a Learning Assistance specialist at the high school level. He is a study skills expert, a brain gymnastics coach and a Brain-based learning facilitator. He has presented keynotes, seminars and workshops to thousands of teachers, students, parents, families, professionals and the general public for many years. His uniquely engaging, energetic presentations are always humorous and full of optimism to support anyone to learn.

Gary presents training on Brain-based learning strategies for early childhood educators, kindergarten, elementary, middle and high school teachers. Workshop themes include:

Growing the Child's Brain
The Magical Teenage Brain
Differentiated Instruction Strategies
Engaging the Student Brain

He is also the author of Brain Wellness The Secrets for Longevity, a self-help guide book offering dozens of practical prevention strategies to avoid cognitive decline. Workshop themes include:

Brain Wellness The Secrets for Longevity
Caring for the Caregiver's Brain
Brain Wellness for Seniors

Contact Gary at
ganaka@telus.net
1-250-753-0688
www.braincoach.ca